P9-DCC-256

Scotch and *Toilet Water?*

"*Scotch and toilet water?*"

Scotch and *Toilet Water?*

A Book of Dog Cartoons

by Leo Cullum

Harry N. Abrams, Inc., Publishers

ACKNOWLEDGMENTS

Thanks to Lee Lorenz, Bob Mankoff, Jane Cavolina,
Christopher Sweet, the people at the Cartoon Bank,
and all the great dogs I ever knew.

Editor: Christopher Sweet
Designer: Robert McKee
Production Manager: Maria Pia Gramaglia

Library of Congress Cataloging-in-Publication Data

Cullum, Leo.
 Scotch and toilet water? : a book of dog cartoons /
by Leo Cullum.
  p. cm.
 ISBN 0-8109-4439-1
 1. Dogs—Caricatures and cartoons.
 2. American wit and humor,
Pictorial. I. Title.

NC1429.C84 A4 2003
741.5'973—dc21
         2002015523

Copyright © 2003 Leo Cullum
Published in 2003 by Harry N. Abrams, Incorporated, New York.
All rights reserved. No part of the contents of this book may be
reproduced without written permission of the publisher.

Printed and bound in China

10 9 8 7 6 5 4 3

Harry N. Abrams, Inc.
100 Fifth Avenue
New York, N.Y. 10011
www.abramsbooks.com

Abrams is a subsidiary of

"I can't explain it. I see that guy coming up the walkway and I go postal."

For Kathy, Kimberly, and Kaitlin, with love

"*Bad news. The mailman is going to attend the parole-board hearing.*"

"Well, your nose feels cold."

Introduction

Somewhere in the misty recesses of time (long, long ago), a wolf approached a tribe's campfire and accepted a cookie from a man, or perhaps a woman. This was the beginning of the domestic dog. This wolf-dog then proceeded to bite the mailman from another tribe. This was the beginning of a cliché.

My own relationship with dogs began in the early 1950s with "Mugsy," a dog who just showed up, which is how I acquired several dogs. Other dogs were Snowy, Cokie, Bozo, Kuku, Sushi, Calypso, Lulu, and Winnie. I didn't choose all the names, just the cool ones. Our current main dog is Winnie, a gift to one of my daughters from a family friend. She is a yellow lab, and a better trainer of humans would be hard to find. She paws my leg, I scratch her ear. She barks, I let her in (or out, depending on which side of the door she is on). She brings the paper, I give her a cookie. She gets dirty, I bathe her. She also serves as inspiration for many of my cartoons. Labs are easy to draw, not having many sharp edges, just a general amorphous shape, which editors seem to agree is a dog. If she could understand what was going on, she might be offended, but I'm certain she would realize it is all an effort to put food on the table, which then trickles down to that smorgasbord under the table.

I do drawings on a variety of subjects, but dogs seem to be a recurrent theme, even if it is a cartoon about something else cleverly disguised as a dog cartoon. Thus a dog may wind up at a bar wearing a bespoke suit and drinking a martini. Certainly, the martini is possible, but the suit is a stretch. The dog becomes a vehicle to snipe at attorneys, accountants, businessmen, and anyone else smarter and more industrious than a cartoonist. This, however, is done with the same affection I have for my dog when drawing cartoons about her. So I say to the offended attorney, "Lie down. Have a cookie!"

I often find my dog with furrowed brow sprawled on the kitchen floor, which causes me to ask, "What the heck is going on in that dog's head? Anything? Nothing? What?" Perhaps it is the ennui that comes with the realization she has not fulfilled her hunting destiny. Our other dog, Lulu, a cocker spaniel, doesn't seem to have these regrets. She was bred to tear paper into small scraps and is the picture of contentment. But I could never ask Winnie to risk her health by plunging into an icy bay in search of a mortally wounded duck. Unless, it were for a beer commercial. Then count us in—I'll fetch the duck myself.

In terms of life span, dogs seem to live in a parallel universe. Using the dog-years-to-human-years formula, I have discovered that Winnie and I are now the same age, and she will rapidly pass me, becoming an oracle from my future with all its aches and pains. Her message and mine would be the same: Keep us comfortable.

—Leo Cullum, 2002

"You're going to do time, but I'm trying to get it in dog years."

"Bill did the voice-over for this commercial."

"*Selective breeding has given me an aptitude for the law, but I still love fetching a dead duck out of freezing water.*"

"Have you considered the possibility that I don't _want_ the paper?"

"They don't keep YOU on a leash because they WANT you to run away."

"Thanks for waiting for me, Jocko, but I still can't play. I've decided to go for a Ph.D."

"Your disapproval rating is now 100%."

"Ha! You were taking a catnap!"

"*I heard the call of the wild once, but it was right before the bar exam.*"

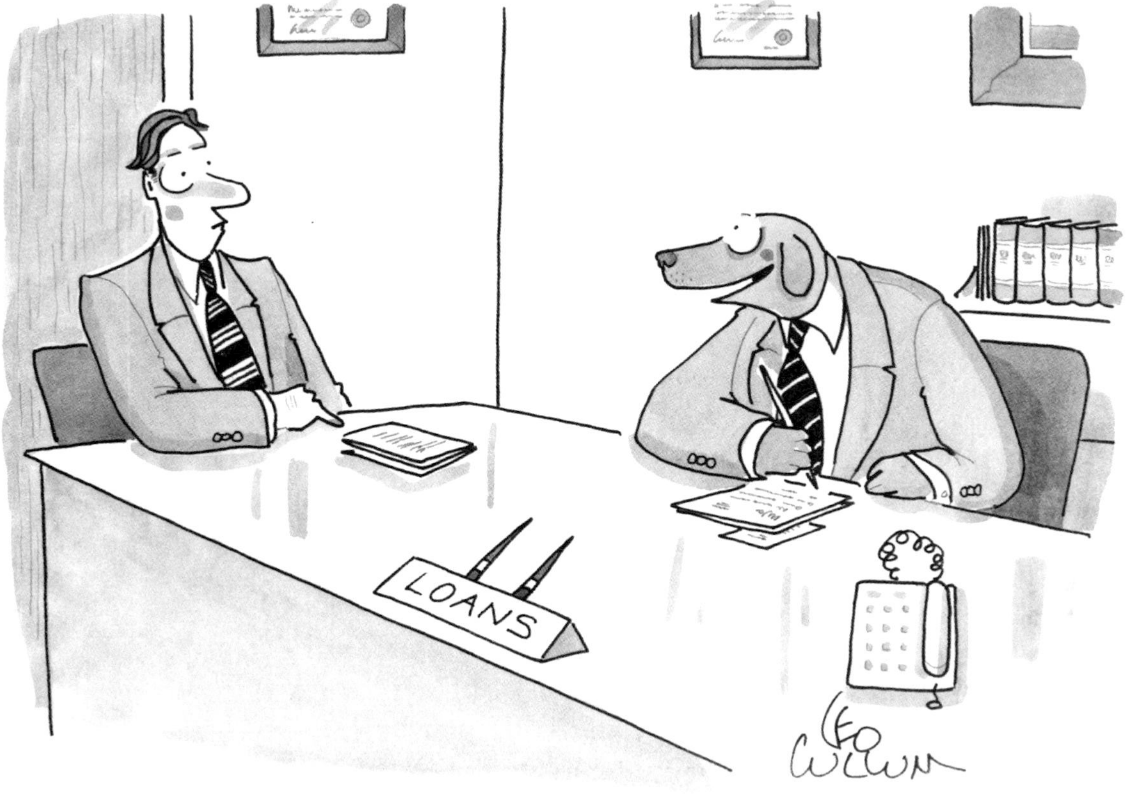
LOANS

"Well,. . . you smell honest."

"I'm going to disqualify myself."

"This isn't haiku. This is doggerel!"

"*Cut that out!*"

"It's absolutely true. One Fedex driver is equal to three mailmen."

"*Give me five minutes. I'll have him eating out of my hand.*"

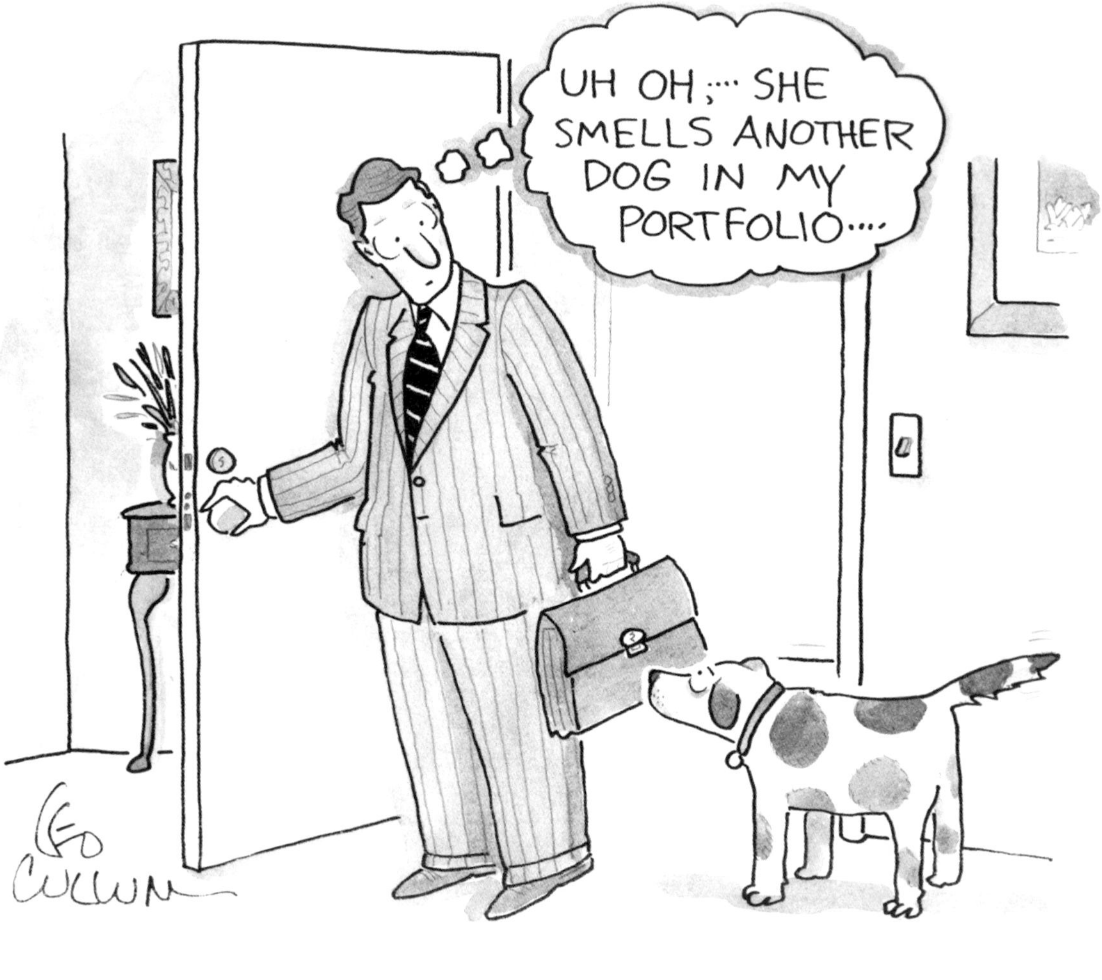
UH OH;... SHE SMELLS ANOTHER DOG IN MY PORTFOLIO....
LEO CULLUM

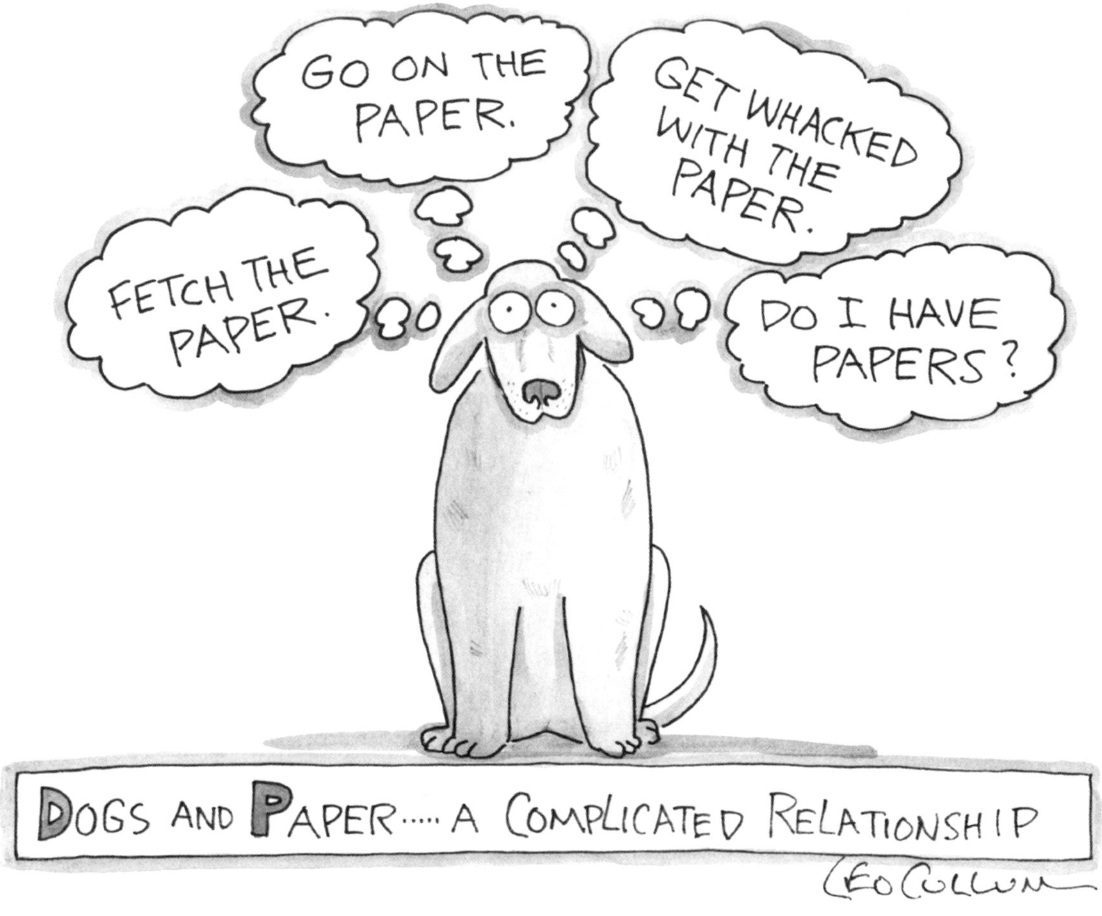
GO ON THE PAPER.
GET WHACKED WITH THE PAPER.
FETCH THE PAPER.
DO I HAVE PAPERS?
DOGS AND PAPER..... A COMPLICATED RELATIONSHIP
LEO CULLUM

"I'm licensed in New York, Connecticut and Florida."

"Remember, Cogswell, if you need to see me, I have an open door policy."

"I love the new title, I love the new salary and I love the new office,
but mostly I love hanging my head out that window."

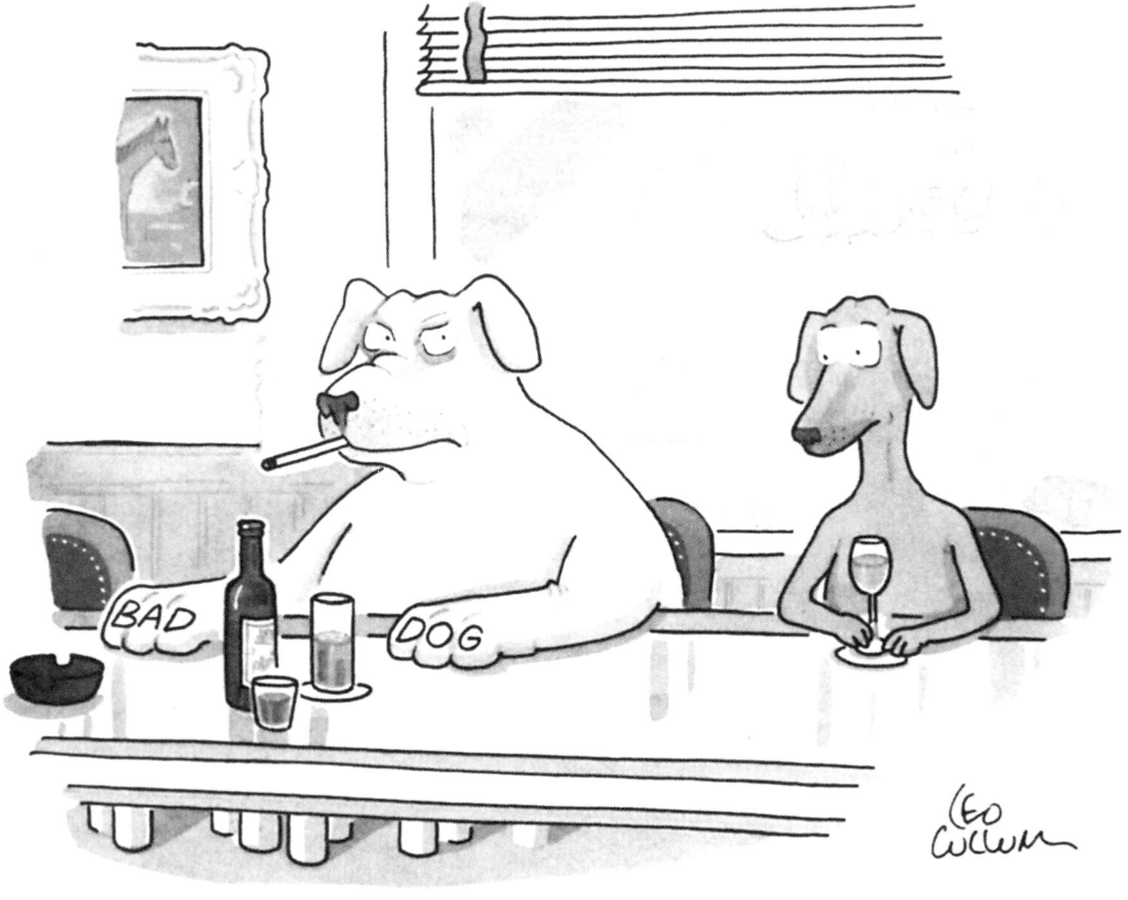
BAD
DOG
LEO CULLUM

"I liked it better when it was a 'dog eat cat' world."

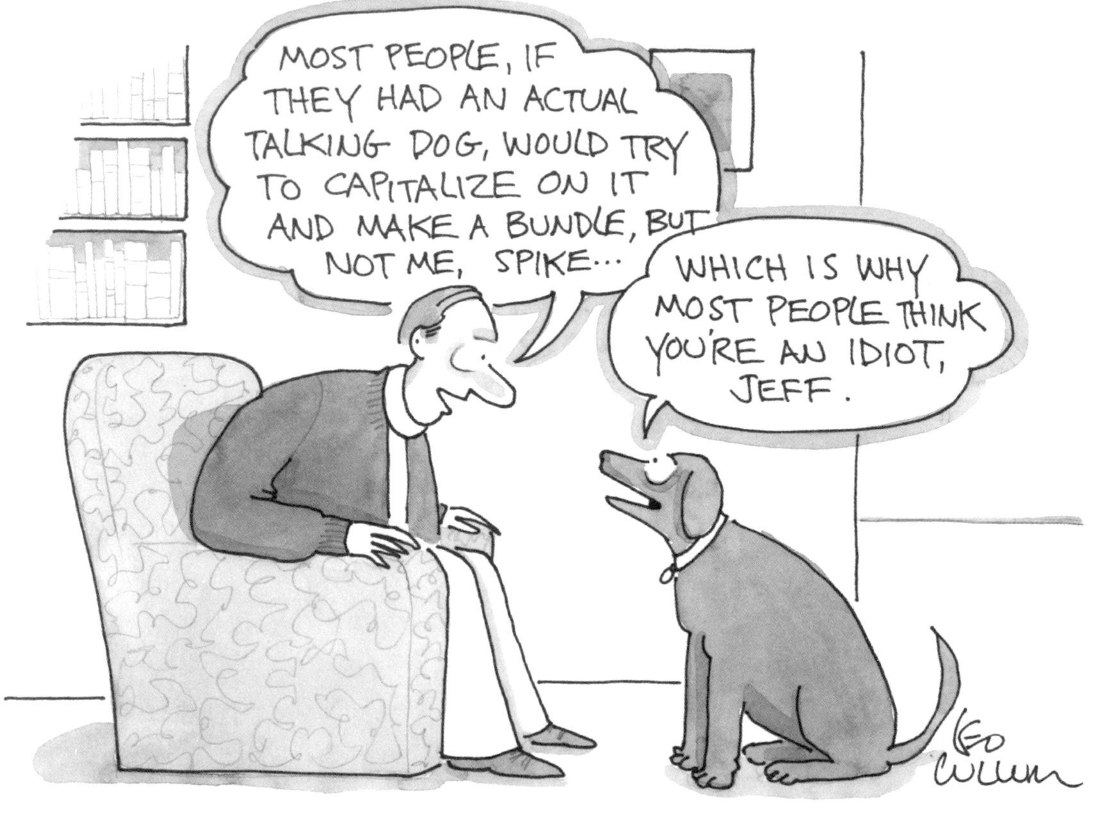
MOST PEOPLE, IF THEY HAD AN ACTUAL TALKING DOG, WOULD TRY TO CAPITALIZE ON IT AND MAKE A BUNDLE, BUT NOT ME, SPIKE...
WHICH IS WHY MOST PEOPLE THINK YOU'RE AN IDIOT, JEFF.
LEO CULLUM

"*There you go with that typical police mentality.*"

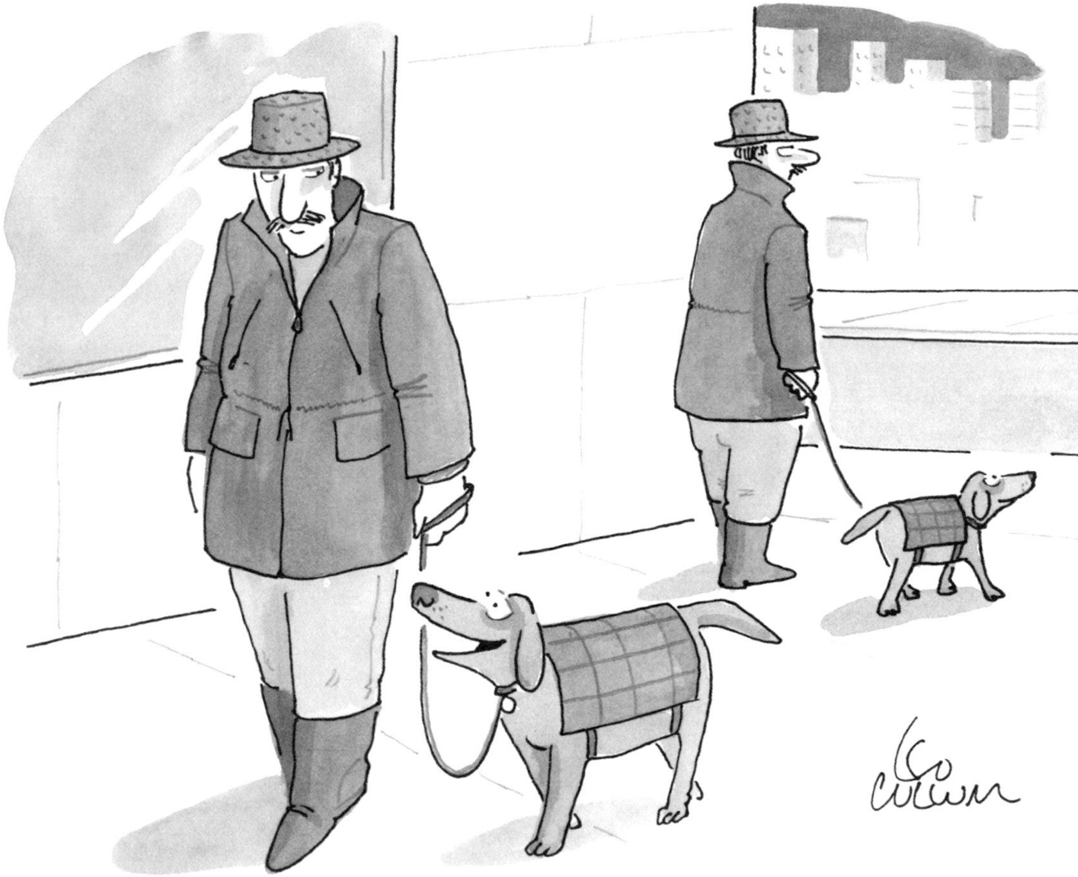
Leo Cullum

"I like them."

"You've got to understand, in my family Dad was the poodle and Mom was the pit bull."

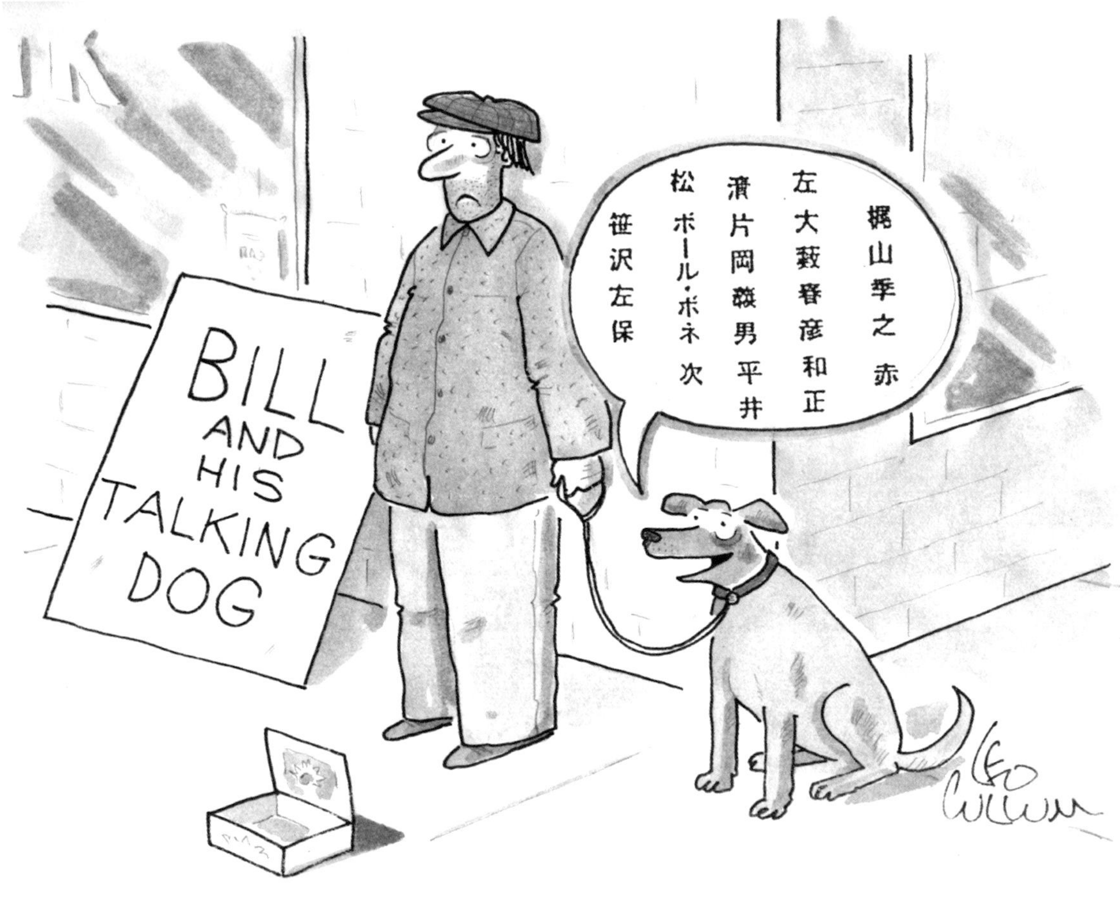
BILL AND HIS TALKING DOG
梶山季之 赤
左大藪春彦和正
濱片岡義男平井
松ボール・ボネ次
笹沢左保

"Could you give me a moment? I just had nine puppies."

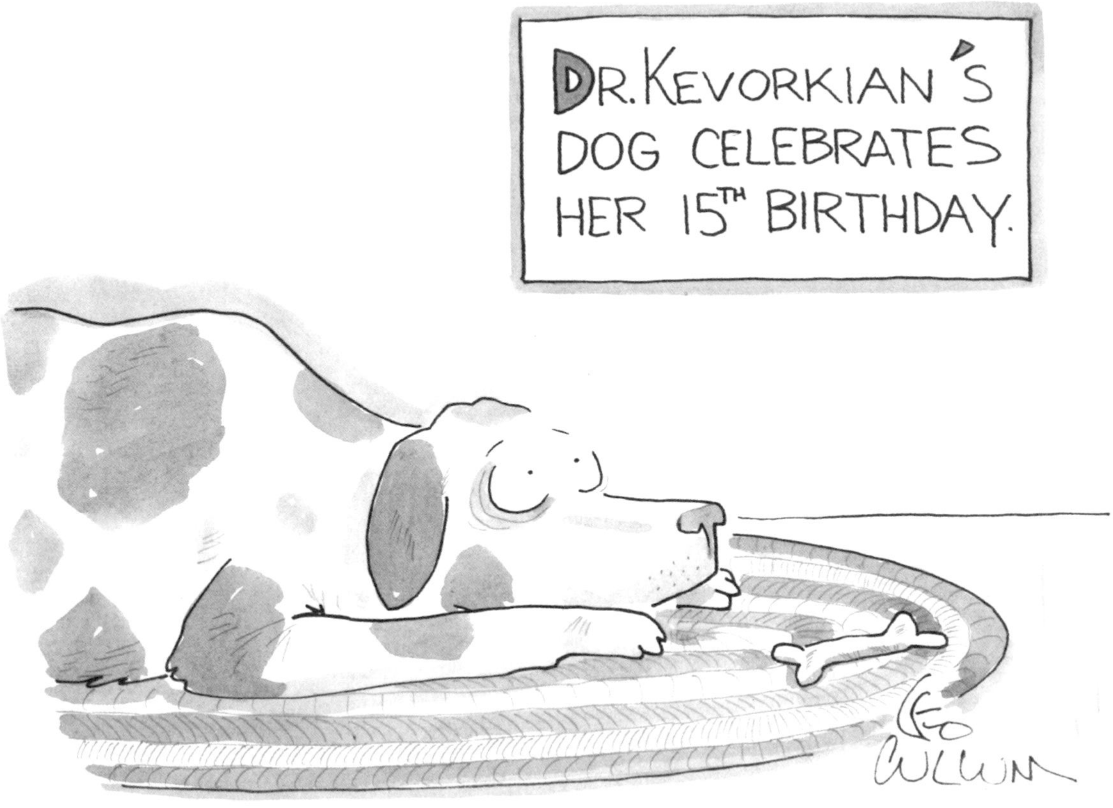
DR. KEVORKIAN'S
DOG CELEBRATES
HER 15TH BIRTHDAY.

"*Just how many ways <u>are</u> there to skin a cat?*"

"For the girls—Kimberly, Caitlin, Lauren, Cindy, and Tracy.
For the boys—Cameron, Christopher, Adam, Jeffrey, and Gregory."

"You could have had a film career, but you were needed here to fetch the paper."

"*The pension fund,…I forgot where I buried it!*"

"The best part about aging seven years for each human year is that we can drink when we're three."

"Face it. For soft shoe you can't beat a cat."

"*They always said I'd be really big, but it turns out that big feet just meant big feet.*"

"I've never done it, but I'd love to bite someone's head off."

"Listen to me, Dave. I'm not just your friend, I'm your veterinarian."

"*We love the lot, but the house is a total teardown.*"

"I learned a new trick yesterday, but I've forgotten it."

"We're fighting like—well, we're fighting."

"I'll be honest, Winnie. I feed you, you lick my face. It's not going to go any further."

"Here's my number. If a man answers, hang up."

"*She's not angry at you, Sushi; she's angry that your paws were muddy.*"

"*I don't see a date of birth.*"

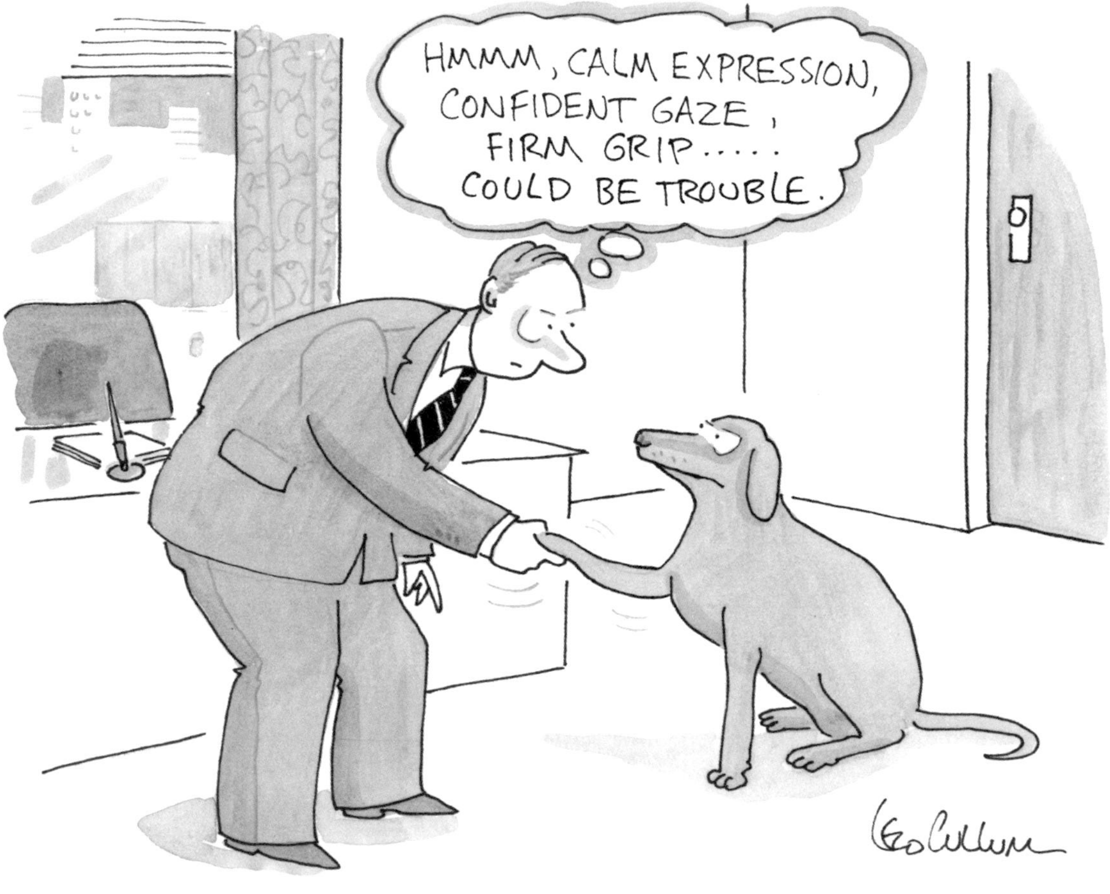
HMMM, CALM EXPRESSION,
CONFIDENT GAZE,
FIRM GRIP.....
COULD BE TROUBLE.

"He was a whistle-blower, but I was the only one who could hear it."

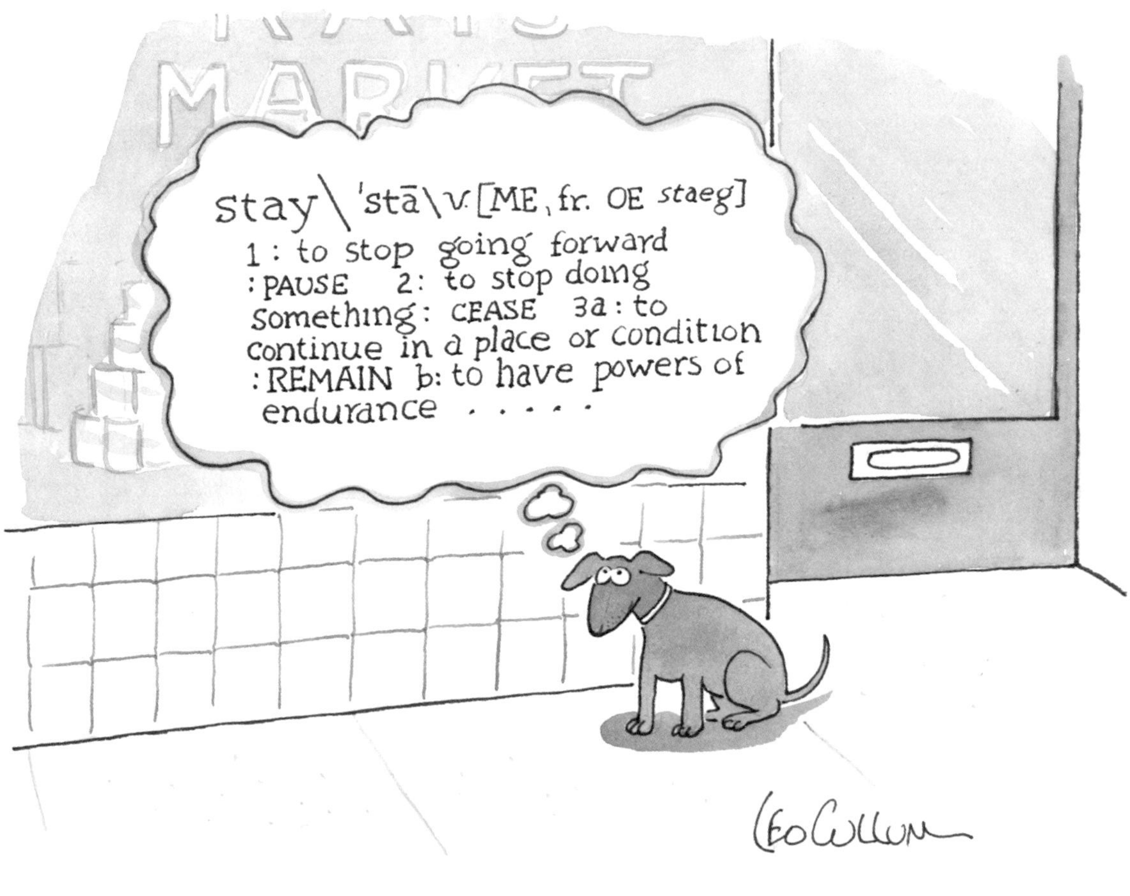
stay \ 'stā \ v. [ME, fr. OE staeg]
1 : to stop going forward : PAUSE 2 : to stop doing something : CEASE 3a : to continue in a place or condition : REMAIN b: to have powers of endurance . . . . .

"I got a lot done this morning, but this afternoon I just chased my tail."

"Like many attorneys, I was the runt of the litter."

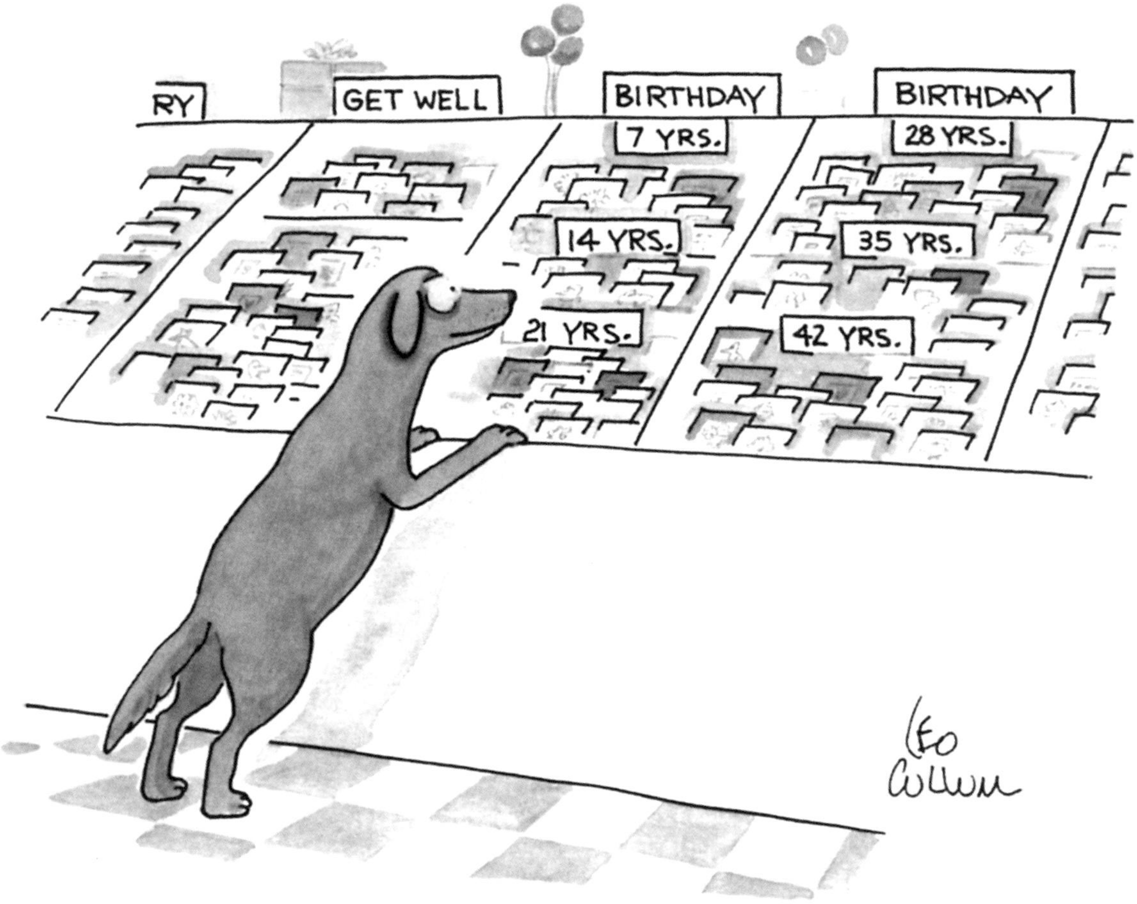
RY
GET WELL
BIRTHDAY
7 YRS.
14 YRS.
21 YRS.
BIRTHDAY
28 YRS.
35 YRS.
42 YRS.

"Thursday's no good. That's my flea bath."

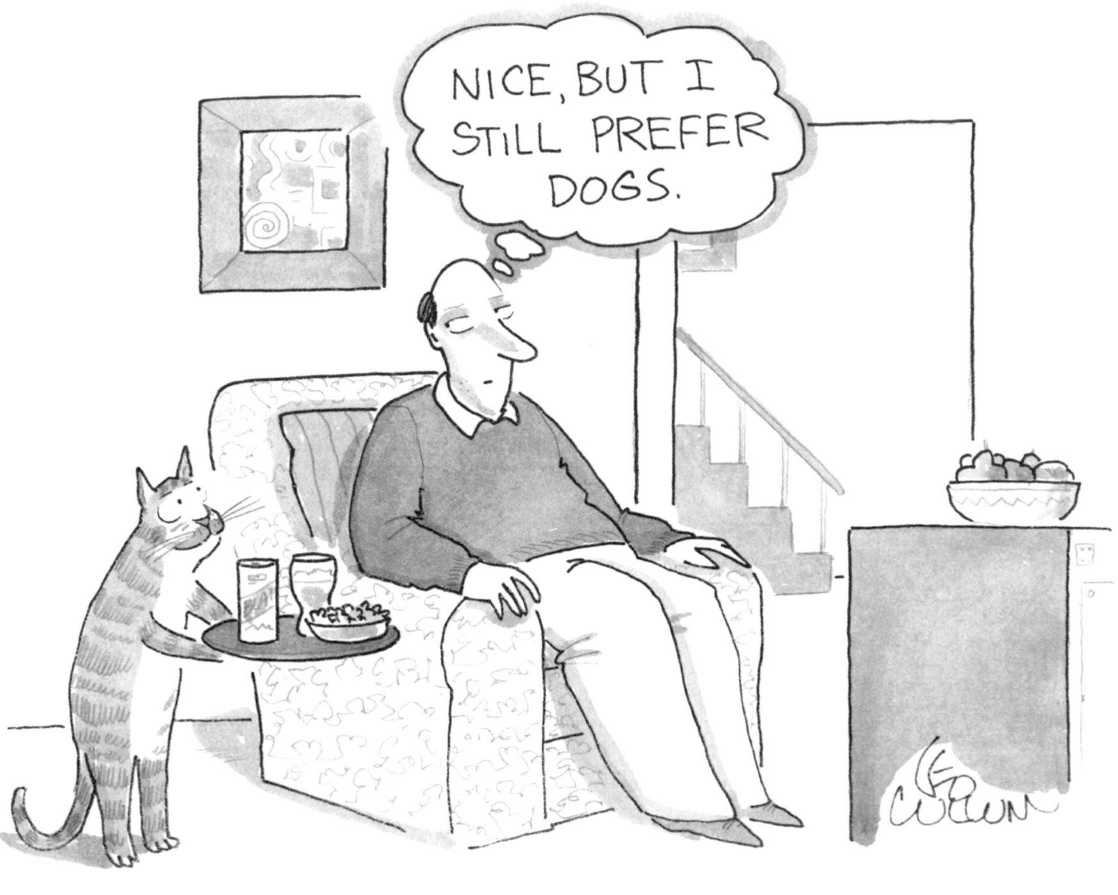
NICE, BUT I STILL PREFER DOGS.

"I'm a purebred, but they don't have the papers."

"I have to tell you, you were not my first choice for this job."

"Sirius…Ha! The Dog Star!"

"I think he's trying to tell us something, Ted."

"Are you still working on that?"

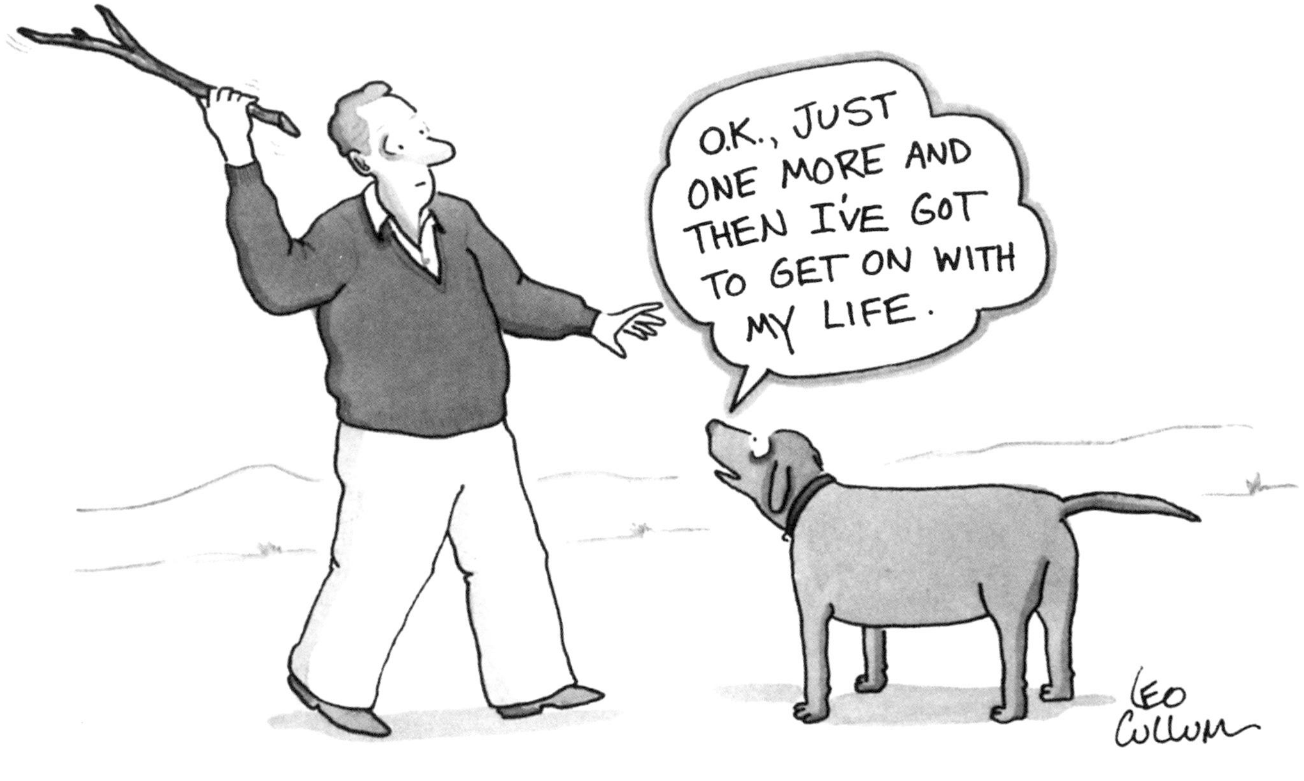
O.K., JUST ONE MORE AND THEN I'VE GOT TO GET ON WITH MY LIFE.
LEO CULLUM

"*You were a lot more effective, Hargrove, before you were neutered.*"

"Yes, you're my best friend, and no, I'm not lending you forty thousand dollars."

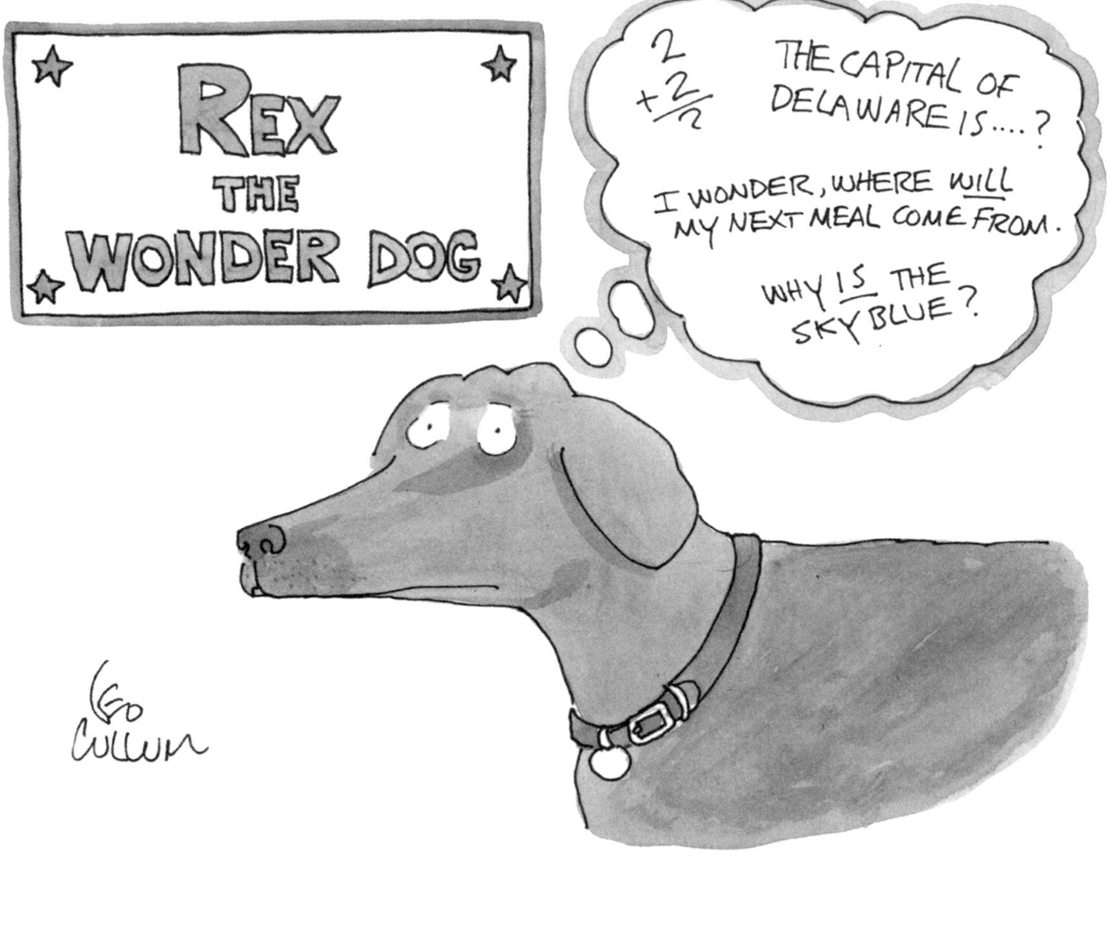

REX
THE
WONDER DOG
2
+2
?
THE CAPITAL OF
DELAWARE IS....?
I WONDER, WHERE WILL
MY NEXT MEAL COME FROM.
WHY IS THE
SKY BLUE?
LEO CULLUM

"It's got hardly any closet space, but then, I only have three collars."

"They could housebend me, but they couldn't housebreak me."

"*Someday, and I'm very serious about this, your picture could be up there.*"

"He's French. Need I say more?"

"*You're kidding, right?*"

"I just got married."

"*It's genetic. My father was a dog, and I'm a dog.*"

"You're kidding! I think I'm from Labrador, too."

"Get loud and cause a scene and you're back on the leash."

"*I don't know anything about the Stockholm Syndrome. I just think he's cute.*"

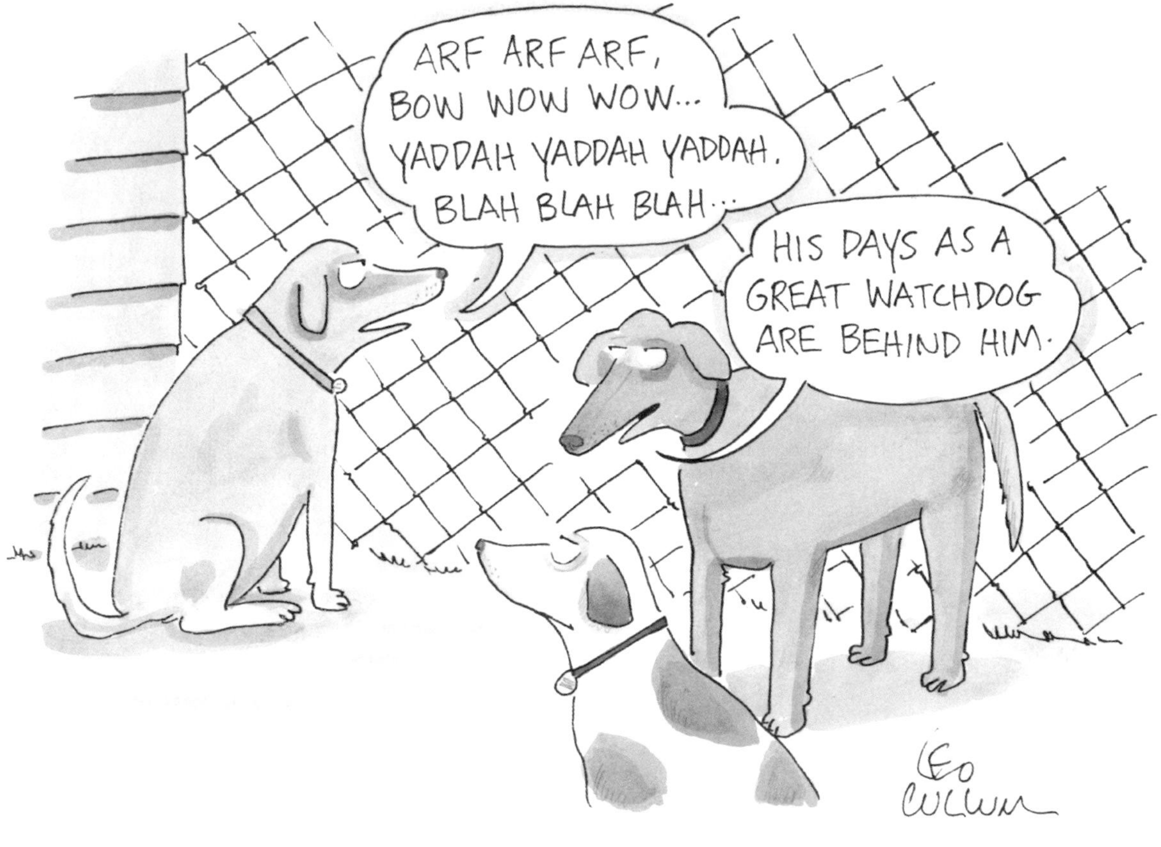

ARF ARF ARF, BOW WOW WOW... YADDAH YADDAH YADDAH, BLAH BLAH BLAH...
HIS DAYS AS A GREAT WATCHDOG ARE BEHIND HIM.
LEO CULLUM

"*I'm <u>very</u> territorial, which is odd, because we live in a condo.*"

"Eat! Drink! Be Merry!"

"You're needed at the cookie jar."

"Daisy is my married name. It was also my maiden name."

"Yes, Doreen, I think I _am_ capable of unconditional love."

"Remember, this is just an experiment."

"'Fido.' It means 'I am faithful,' which of course I'm not."

"*Originally we were bred to tear paper into tiny scraps, but now we mostly bark at nothing.*"

"*I do like it here, but I'm ready for my own apartment.*"

"*Really? Everyone we hang out with we also met through our puppies.*"

"You've got to have something to fall back on. Me...I'm a licensed pet."

"The previous department head gave us little treats."

"*I bit someone once. It tasted like chicken.*"

"You only *think* you're barking at nothing. We're *all* barking at *something*."

"He bought one of those silent dog whistles today. Pretend to hear it."

"First of all, forget everything you learned in obedience school."

"Oh, he's funny, but not 'woof woof' funny."

"I know you're a working dog, Angus. I just don't have anything for you right now."

"*It's not enough that we succeed. Cats must also fail.*"

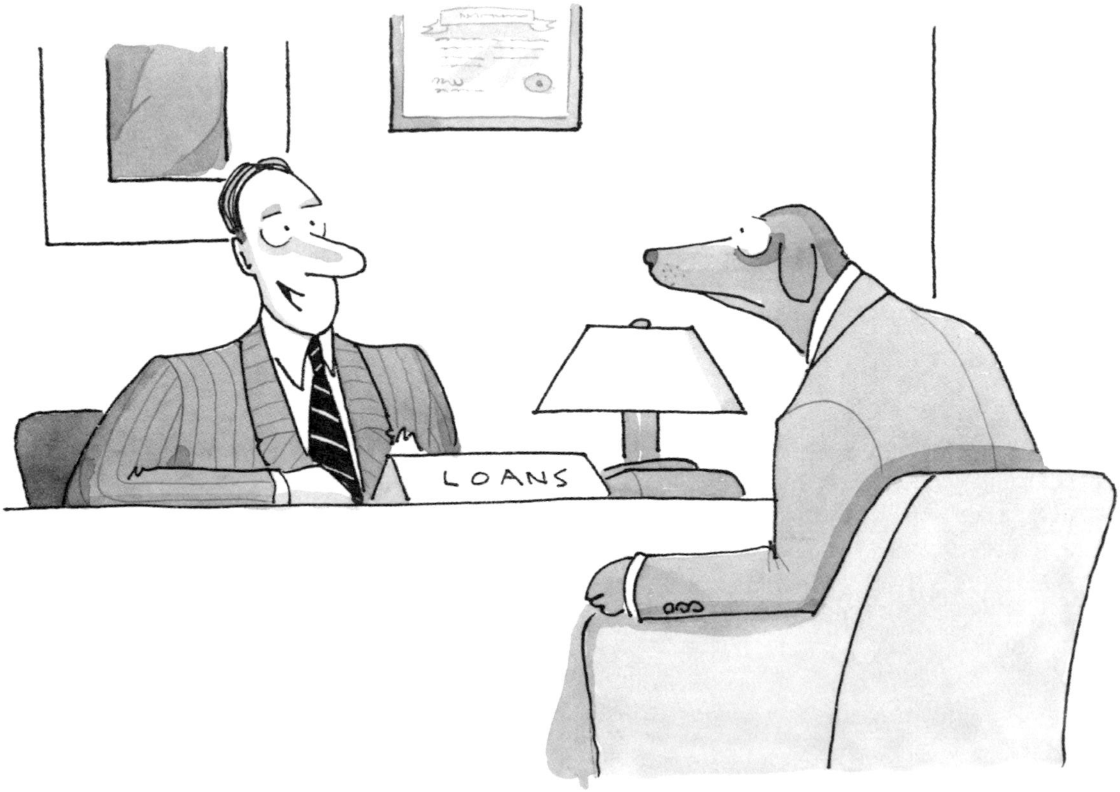
LOANS

"Beg."

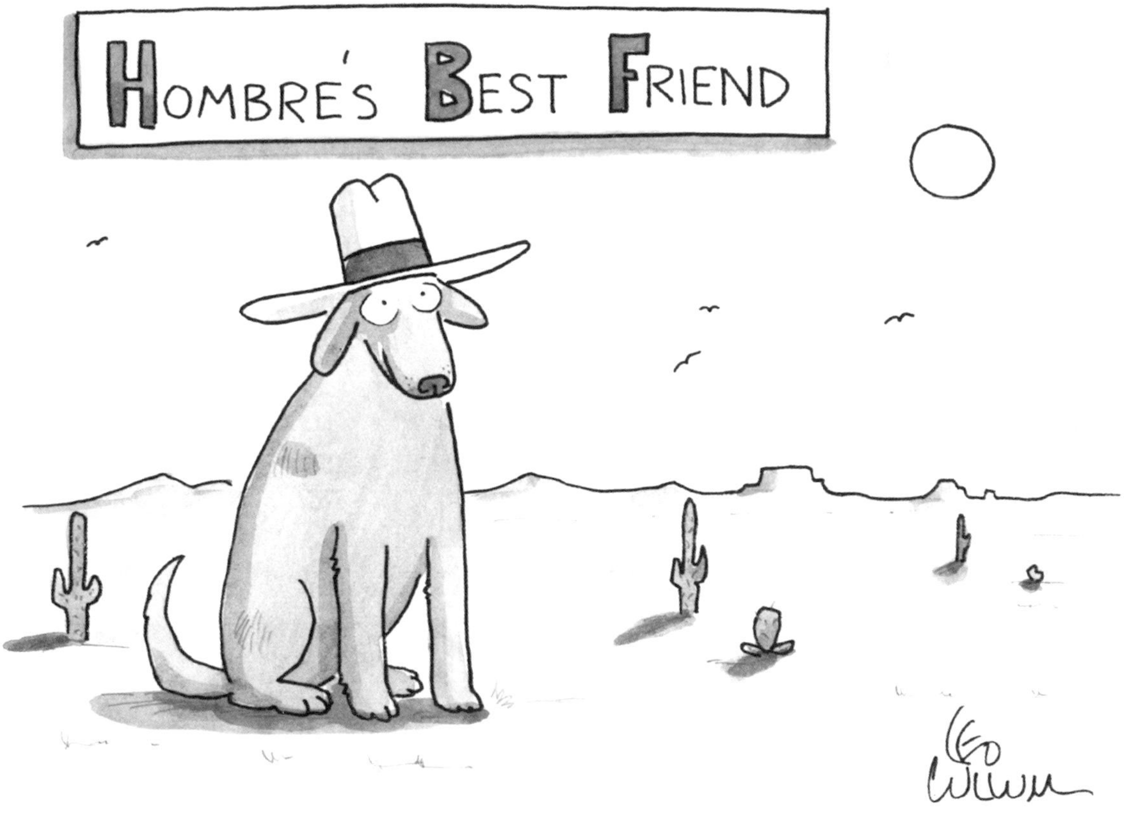
HOMBRE'S BEST FRIEND

"*Whenever I have those icky thoughts, I just put them in a little box and bury it in the yard.*"

"It's just the architect's model, but I'm very excited."

"Oscar and I have decided not to have puppies. The world is already full of annoying little dogs."

"You've been with us a long time, Winnie, and we're prepared to offer you a generous severance package."

"Did you know you move your lips when you read?"

"O.K., I messed up. He didn't have to rub my nose in it."

"Honey,…Oscar wants to go for a walk."

"An Oldsmobile? My Larry was hit by a Mercedes-Benz."

"I said 'bring me the papers,' Hayward, not 'bring me the paper.'"

"If I promised not to try anything funny, would you loosen my collar a bit?"

"*I understand that seventy-five percent of those who've been in the pound eventually wind up back there.*"

"Then he said 'bark like a dog,' and I said 'can do.'"

"I've come to the realization I'm just a trophy dog."

"*Don't ask questions, Maureen. If I say I need to go out, I need to go out.*"

"We really miss Arnold, don't we, Rex?"

"I've had sixty-seven puppies and every one of them went to obedience school."

"And you never wondered <u>why</u> they call me 'Rover'?"

"*Your feet are wet because someone neglected to rub mink oil on your boots.*"

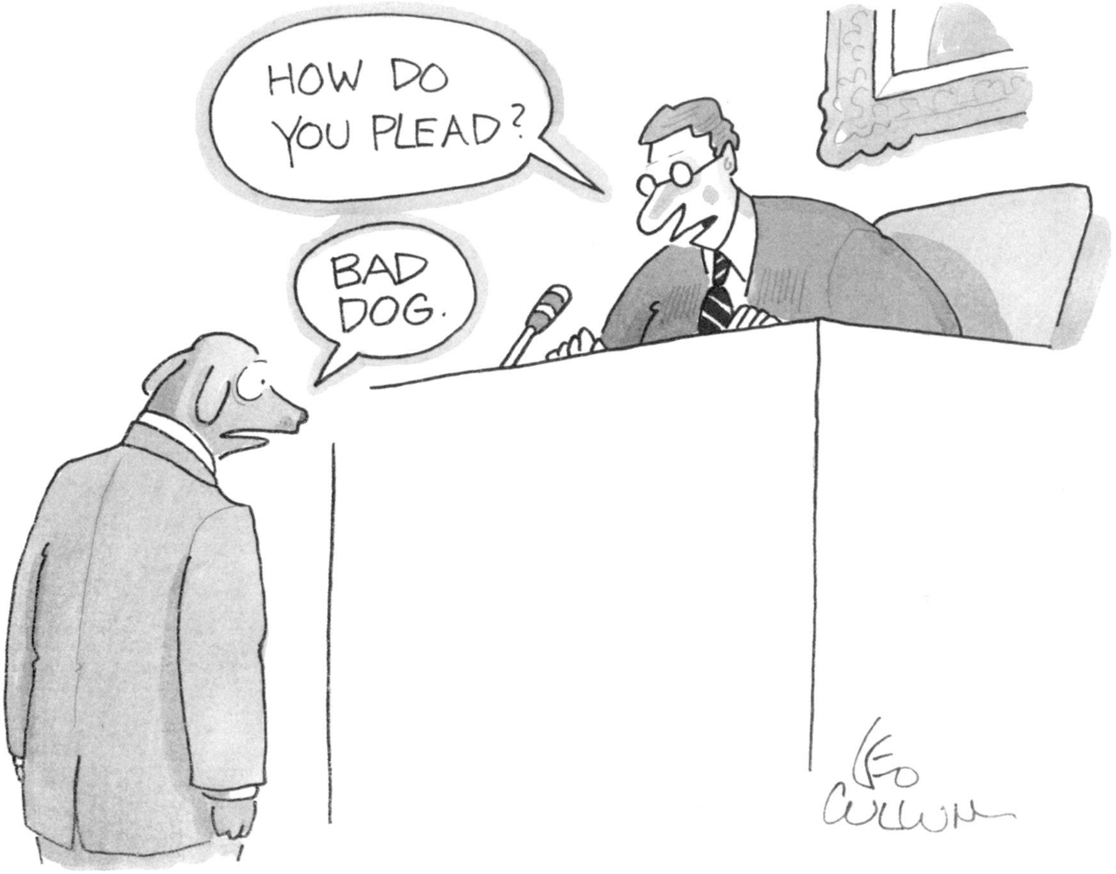
HOW DO YOU PLEAD?
BAD DOG.

"I don't bug you about your catnip. Don't bug me about my Martinis."

"Remember, the enemy of your enemy is your friend."

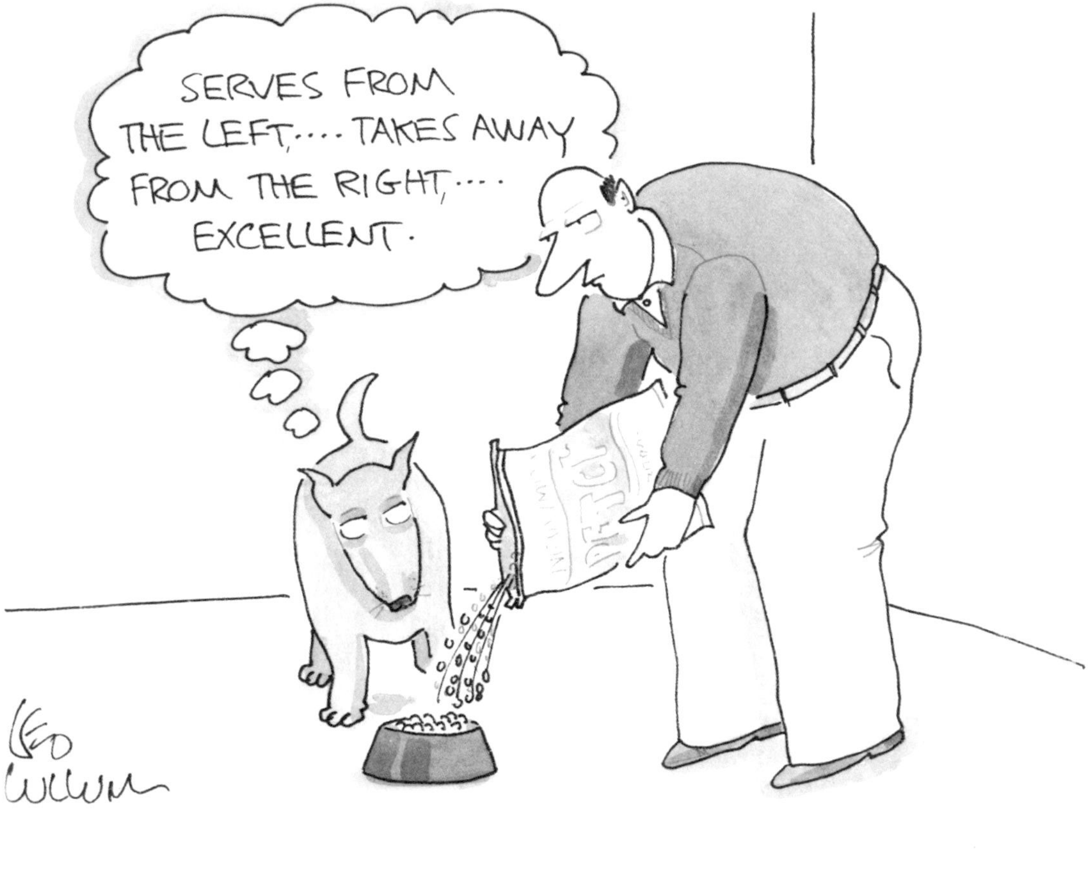
SERVES FROM THE LEFT,.... TAKES AWAY FROM THE RIGHT,.... EXCELLENT.

"*I can't believe he's that old. He must have been drinking from the toilet bowl of youth.*"